EMMITT SMITH

TRIUMPH
BOOKS
CHICAGO

Contributors

Linc Wonham ... Editor
Ray Ramos ... Designer

Photography
AP/Wide World Photo
Allsport
David Durochik/SportPics
Tom DiPace

This book is available in quantity at special discounts for your group or organization. For further information, contact:

Triumph Books
601 South LaSalle Street
Suite 500
Chicago, Illinois 60605
(312) 939-3330
Fax (312) 663-3557

Printed in the United States of America

ISBN: 1-57243-544-5

Contents

The Milestone

Home fans witness history during 109-yard performance

He didn't just sneak in there. The run that made Emmitt Smith the most prolific running back in National Football League history was a dive play gone good.

Smith hit the hole opened by the Dallas Cowboys' offensive line and chugged to an 11-yard gain. Even as he broke into daylight Smith knew that this was the one that would nudge him past the late, great Walter Payton to become the league's all-time leading rusher.

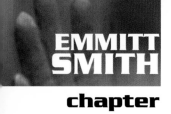

chapter

1

THE MILESTONE

Payton had once explained that his aim in amassing more than 16,000 yards was "to set the record so high that the next person who tries for it, it's going to bust their heart."

Smith, though, had long shown the ample heart necessary for the task. The all-time rushing title was a goal that he had set before his rookie season, and it had taken him 13 years to reach it, the same number of seasons it had taken Payton.

"I was counted out many times in my 13 years here, and I'm probably still counted out," Smith said. "But I believe truly in my own ability. I believe my talent stacks up with the next man."

Eddie Payton, brother of Walter Payton, was on hand to celebrate with the NFL's new all-time career rushing leader on October 27, 2002, in Irving, Texas.

"I'm very confident I'm one of the best to ever play the game, but once you talk about the greatest, how can you define greatest?"

One good place to start is to match performance with personal character. Emmitt, like the man whose record he eclipsed, fares well in those categories. Typical of the Smith that his legion of fans has come to appreciate, he used the record-breaking occasion to honor Payton's memory while celebrating his own achievement.

"Today is a special day for me, my family, and the Payton family," the 33-year-old Smith told a throng of cheering fans at Texas Stadium. "Without Walter Payton doing what he did in the National Football League and representing all he represented, he wouldn't have given a young man like myself a dream, something to shoot after, and a person to look up to and try to emulate in every way possible."

By the end of his most memorable day, Smith had rolled his total to 16,743 career yards and seemed a sure bet to pad that number over the remainder of the 2002 season. Payton closed his career in 1987 with 16,726.

Statisticians point out that Payton reached his mark in 193 games while Smith got there in 196, indicating just how closely these two men share the stature and accomplishment.

On hand to see the game from a box in Texas Stadium were Payton's mother, Alyne, and brother, Eddie. Payton's widow, Connie, sent her congratulations via videotape. "I am so proud of you, Emmitt," Connie Payton said in the message. "Your hard work and determination, your being true to the game, are a part of your success. I feel we're truly blessed having you as a friend and part of our life."

She confirmed that Smith had displayed the necessary heart—so great a heart, in fact, that Payton himself would have cheered the effort. The two backs became friends in the early nineties when Emmitt was a brilliant young player

Smith is lifted by fullback Robert Thomas after breaking the record with an 11-yard run in the fourth quarter.

turning the league on its ear with his presence, and Payton was the game's elder statesman, imbued with the class and warmth emblematic of his nickname, "Sweetness."

When Payton was dying of cancer in 1999 at age 45, he urged his son Jarrett to become friends with Smith, which has led to a strong relationship between the two. The nature of that strong feeling became apparent in the summer of 2002 when the Payton Foundation honored Emmitt with the second Spirit of Sweetness Award.

THE MILESTONE

"I see myself as a blue-collar worker, a guy who came to work every day and worked hard," Smith said at the time. "I have played so long because I love the game. I could never walk away saying I have shortchanged myself, that I have cheated this sport, that I have disappointed my teammates. I want to look them in the eye and know that they know I gave everything I had."

Giving it everything he had included the ability to display toughness while protecting his body from the hits and ravages that have destroyed many other running backs long before their time. This understanding of self-preservation was as important to Smith as it was to Payton.

"I can remember him taking only two flush hits in his career," recalled Daryl Johnston, the former Cowboy fullback who opened many holes for Smith. "You'd think all the tackles would have taken a toll on his knees and his shoulders, but he can see so well and has such great feel that he can avoid the bad hits. It is amazing."

As the seasons unfolded, Smith became a great student of the game, spending the necessary hours studying tape to find ways of thriving and surviving against each week's defensive challenge.

Although he seems surprisingly slight in person, the key to his physical prowess is his thighs, which afford him the strength to find his way, especially as opposing defenses pack more and more players into the box each week to stop him. Added to that are his shiftiness, his vision, and his subtle probing of his opportunities as each running play takes shape.

"But it takes more than natural talent to be the best in those moments," Norv Turner, the former Cowboys offensive coordinator, told *The Sporting News*. "You have to want to do it. And Emmitt wants to do more than anyone I have ever been around. You just don't develop that kind of heart. You show up with it."

That heart helped boost Emmitt over the fall of 2002 as he stretched to chase Sweetness, an effort that culminated on October 27 against the Seattle Seahawks. As the weeks peeled away and Smith moved closer and closer to Payton's record, it became clear that the Seahawks game, which came at the end of a run of October home games, would be the likely place he would reach his mark—in front of the fans that have worshipped him for 13 seasons.

THE MILESTONE

The Seahawks seemed a promising opponent with their struggling start to the season. The Cowboys needed this win to even their record at 4–4. Emmitt did his part early on by rushing for 55 yards in the first quarter. He netted 15 of those on the Cowboys' first three plays.

Then came that nasty second period that produced his first fumble in almost a year and two other running plays that lost yardage.

The third period brought a turnaround. Emmitt's five rushes for 25 yards helped sustain a drive to tie the score at 7–all. But

Seattle rolled back into the lead, 14–7, and the sense of urgency in Texas Stadium seemed to meld with the anticipation.

Emmitt stood just 13 yards from the mark when Dallas took over at its own 27 in the fourth. The scene provided a strobe of popping flash bulbs when Emmitt dove inside tackle for three yards.

On the next play he took a handoff and headed left to find a hole opened by Flozell Adams and Jeremy McKinney. "Once I broke the line of scrimmage, I knew that had to be the one," Smith said later.

He steadied himself after tripping through a tangle of arms and rolled on for the 11-yard gain that broke the record. The game paused there as Emmitt stopped to hug family and friends and hail the crowd, but the bulk of the celebration would be saved for afterward.

With the resumption of play, he closed out the drive with a one-yard scoring plunge that tied the game at 14–all.

The sense that the day would produce an absolutely storybook comeback died minutes later when Seattle drove into field-goal range and Rian Lindell booted a 20-yarder with 25 seconds left. The Seahawks had dampened Emmitt's big day with a 17–14 win.

The Cowboys acknowledged their mix of dismay and delight, the latter highlighted with a postgame celebration of the record.

Smith had closed out the day with 109 yards on 24 carries, season highs in both categories. His longest run of the day had been 14 yards, and six times he had broken off runs of better than 10 yards. His touchdown had also allowed him to add to his total of 150 rushing TDs, another league record.

"He loves the challenge—the bigger, the better," said Cowboys coach Dave Campo. "That is what is so impressive about him. You need your best players to be at their best in these games, and there is never a doubt about Emmitt—ever."

Career Statistics

Year	G	ATT	YDS	AVG	LG	TD
1990	16	241	937	3.9	48	11
1991	16	365	1,563	4.3	75	12
1992	16	373	1,713	4.6	68	18
1993	14	283	1,486	5.3	62	9
1994	15	368	1,484	4.0	46	21
1995	16	377	1,773	4.7	60	25
1996	15	327	1,204	3.7	42	12
1997	16	261	1,074	4.1	44	4
1998	16	319	1,332	4.2	32	13
1999	15	329	1,397	4.2	63	11
2000	16	294	1,203	4.1	52	9
2001	14	261	1,021	3.9	44	3
2002*	8	131	556	4.2	30	2
TOTALS*	193	3,929	16,743	4.3	75	150

* Through October 27, 2002

A savvy sports marketer, Smith took the opportunity to change jerseys and shoes before each quarter along with a white T-shirt commemorating his accomplishment. This would provide him supply enough for the Hall of Fame, for the collectibles market, and for his own memorabilia.

"He is an intriguing combination of cockiness and humbleness and wants to leave behind remarkable footprints," noted Paul Attner of *The Sporting News*.

The postgame ceremony brought smoke rising around a huge, inflated helmet. Smith trotted out to greet the crowd in full uniform, sporting a cap that commemorated the mark: "16,727."

Smith then ran around the field, taking time to slap hands with fans and savor the moment before Cowboys owner Jerry Jones presented him with a silver football. "There's only one NFL rushing champion, and there's only one Emmitt Smith," Jones told the gathering.

Smith then turned and thanked his family, the crowd, and all involved in his run to glory. "I hope everyone has a chance to enjoy this moment like me," he said.

He tipped his cap afterward and fought back tears when the team dropped a banner from the rafters of Texas Stadium that proclaimed, "All-Time Leading Rusher . . . 22 . . . Emmitt Smith."

"Smith is a strikingly intelligent, aware, media-sophisticated athlete, the perfect man to hold such a storied record," Attner observed. "In this era of sound bites and late-night video highlights, he is a comfortable fit. His smile is captivating, his guts venerable, his grace under adversity admirable."

"Forget what he looks like now," *Sports Illustrated*'s Paul Zimmerman said of a Smith who has battled past his prime to gain the record. "Remember, instead, what he used to be: a dynamic little cutback runner with an explosive power burst. He lasted almost a whole career without a significant backup to share the load. The Cowboys would use him to close out a game and protect a lead, and he became energized as the defense sagged. His courage is legendary."

Despite the disappointment of the loss, Dallas rookie quarterback Chad Hutchinson, making his first career start, talked of what an honor it had been to play a role in Smith getting the record, even if it was just handing off as Emmitt worked to get the job done.

The Seattle defense had stacked its main effort in the box to stop Emmitt, Hutchinson said, and still they hadn't stopped him. "I'll never forget it," Hutchinson said.

And neither would millions of Cowboys fans across Texas and around the country.

For so long Smith had delivered, and now it had paid off. Smith said he wished everyone could experience what he had—but in more ways than one, they had.

He had given them Super Bowl championships and a thousand other memories to treasure. And now he had given them his ultimate prize, the all-time rushing record, the product of his long road to glory.

Smith holds up a silver football trophy given to him by Cowboys owner Jerry Jones after setting the NFL's new career rushing record.

The Man

Few others have shown as much heart on and off the field

Emmitt.

Say the name with me.

Emmitt.

It's a magical word in Cowboy Nation, denoting all that is good about America's Team and conjuring up images of No. 22 roaming Texas Stadium. And Emmitt Smith's stardom with the team that wears the star is such that his first name alone suffices in the overcrowded world of sports superstars.

Few superstars, though, boast the all-star resume that Emmitt Smith has put together in his professional career: Super Bowl championships, rushing titles, records, honors, MVP awards, and a stadium's worth of respect from teammates, opponents, and fans.

THE MAN

Just the name *Emmitt* brings a smile to the lips of Dallas fans, or a knowing nod from NFL aficionados. And it's been that way for 13 years now, ever since he burst upon the scene for America's Team.

Over that span Emmitt has piled up more yards and more touchdowns on the ground than any player in NFL history. He has been at the center of more Cowboy highlights than John Wayne. He is America's running back.

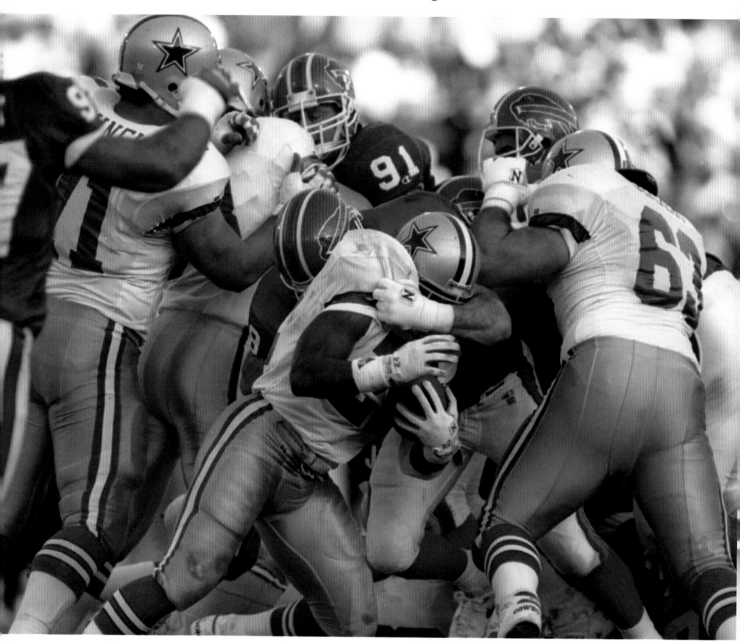

Smith pushes for yardage in the Cowboys' 52–17 victory over Buffalo in Super Bowl XXVII at the Rose Bowl in Pasadena, California.

The images of Emmitt burned into the brain of diehard Dallas fans are innumerable. Emmitt on one knee in the end zone, pointing skyward to celebrate a score. Stiff-arming an opponent as he squeezes just a little more yardage out of a long run. Taking his pads and No. 22 off after another 100-yard effort during the dynasty days to relax on the bench and flash that smile for national television. Hands running through and ruining Jimmy Johnson's cemented hairdo as the clock runs down in the Super Bowl.

Emmitt has filled the scrapbooks in our minds. Moreover, from the day he showed up in Dallas in 1990, he has acquitted himself with class and dignity, often during times when too many of his teammates were simply being acquitted. Emmitt never tarnished the star on his helmet.

As dependable as he has been on the field, Emmitt has been even more rock solid off of it. A devoted family man and a champion for charitable causes throughout his career, he has never failed to make us proud to root for him and the Cowboys.

Smith has been active in so many children's charities and touched so many lives, those numbers may easily surpass the yardage he has piled up in the NFL. That work officially began in 1986 when he attended the White House as a high school representative for the national anti-drug "Just Say No" campaign. Ironically, that's what Smith has been telling would-be tacklers ever since.

And it's no surprise that Emmitt is so involved with children's charities. He brought a wide-eyed wonder to the football field, a simple joy of competition and team comaraderie that inspires friend and foe alike. Teammates adore him whether he's gaining yardage to win the game or humbling them in a game of dominos in the locker room.

Opponents knock him down and he just keeps getting up. He scores and doesn't embarrass opposing players with a dance or a taunt or a jeer. He must also hold the NFL record for congratulating opponents after a tackle, patting

a behind or sharing a smile. He just plays the game—like few ever have.

The heart and soul of the most recent Dallas dynasty, Emmitt redefined toughness in a sport known for the trait. No Cowboys fan will ever forget the 1993 regular-season finale with the New York Giants when Emmitt set a new standard for athletes pushing themselves.

Dallas' 16–13 overtime victory clinched the NFC East title and earned a banged-up Cowboys squad a bye week in the playoffs. Ultimately that much-needed break would play a huge role in the second straight Super Bowl run for this talented team.

None of it would have been possible without Emmitt, who toted the pigskin 32 times for 168 yards and caught 10 passes for another 61 yards against a staunch New York defense. All in all his 42 touches set a Dallas team record—and the Cowboys needed every one of them to prevail on the hard, cold, frozen turf of Giants Stadium.

Smith accounted for 229 of Dallas' 339 yards of total offense that day and had the team's only touchdown. And he did it all almost literally with one hand tied behind his back. Smith separated a shoulder in the second quarter, taking a hard spill at the end of a 46-yard run.

With the tough Giants defense concentrated on limiting the Cowboys' big-play passing game, the fate of his team fell squarely on Emmitt's aching shoulder. What transpired over the final two quarters and during the overtime period moved the already great Smith into the pantheon of all-time Cowboys heroes. As the Giants came back to overcome a Dallas lead, Smith put himself back in the game.

THE MAN

He had 19 more rushes and seven more catches after the injury. On the game-winning drive alone, he accounted for 41 of the 52 yards the team needed to position Eddie Murray for the 41-yard, title-clinching kick.

"I wanted to do whatever it took to win the game," said Smith, who also wrapped up his third straight league rushing championship that day. "Sometimes the linemen would ask me if I was all right. I'd tell them I was. I lied. I wanted to do what I could. I've heard about guys playing hurt. I wanted to play hurt and be effective."

Even a lie from Emmitt is good.

Team trainers had to help Smith dress after the game because he couldn't lift his right shoulder. Despite painkillers, Smith's chest and shoulder ached so badly that he was in tears on the team flight back to Dallas that night.

The rest of the Cowboys went home to rest. Smith was taken straight to the hospital and began recuperating for the postseason, which would culminate several weeks later with a 132-yard, two-touchdown, Super Bowl MVP performance for Smith against Buffalo. He put off surgery until after another Vince Lombardi trophy was safely tucked away at the Cowboys' Valley Ranch complex.

Little Emmitt Smith—sometimes you wonder how he keeps getting up—carried the ball, the Cowboys, and the hopes of their legion of fans that day in New York, as he has done so often. He seems to have the resiliency of Jim Brown, such a powerful runner that in the grainy highlight films of the late fifties and early sixties he often looks bigger than many of the seemingly lead-footed tacklers pursuing him.

Smith rarely looks bigger than anyone on the modern NFL field other than a kicker, and he often seems slower than anyone but the linemen. He is dwarfed in the Dallas huddle by the huge offensive line that the Cowboys assemble annually to open creases for him. He has never possessed that Gale Sayers speed to allow him to outrun all the huge defensive linemen or cat-quick linebackers and defensive backfield assassins that line up across from him each week with their main goal being just to stop Emmitt Smith.

But perhaps no other back has ever played from his rookie year on with such a natural feel for the game. Emmitt has an innate ability to avoid the big hit and find not only the openings in the line, but also the right angles to avoid defenders' biggest blows, and the perfect spots to surge into tackles to avoid being "decleated."

He seems such an inviting target for defenders at 5'9", 209 pounds—but many of his best moves are so subtle that they're often not even noticeable. He might juke a linebacker with a tilt of his head or an almost imperceptible stutter step.

He turns ever so slightly to take on tacklers in a way that makes them seem to slide off of him, unable to inflict the damage they delight in. And unlike so many of the great highlight-reel runners of the last generation, Smith has most often generated his best runs right up the gut. Success there is the essence of Emmitt: substance over style.

Early in his career it was quick-opening draws and off-tackle plays that shot him into the secondary like a bullet. In more recent years the classic Smith move has been poking out from behind one of his huge linemen—like 6'3", 326-pound Larry Allen—and darting for yardage before the angled pursuit catches him.

Watching Emmitt, your heart is in your throat, looking for the hole he'll pick and the defenders he'll dodge. Each time he takes the ball there's the chance you may see something you've never seen before.

THE MAN

Fans sometimes wince when he breaks into the open field because that's when he seems most vulnerable, about to be tackled from behind. While Smith's durability and longevity have long been his professional calling cards, even the most talented runners are always just one lick away from hanging up the cleats for good.

Smith has rarely run as if that thought ever entered his mind and, as it has turned out, he's had the longest tenure of any of the great backs who have suited up for the Cowboys. Slashing Don Perkins played eight years in Dallas. Swivel-hipped Duane Thomas lasted

If Payton's record was ever to be challenged, few believed it would be by the undersized back from Florida who idolized the Bears great as a child.

ust two. Calvin Hill, with his hurdling style, played six years for the Cowboys before leaving, only to return to the team in recent years as a consultant. The Cowboy's Cowboy, Walt Garrison, played nine years from 1966–1974, running like a pinball bouncing off the bumpers. Robert Newhouse, he of the NFL's largest thighs, played 12 years and is best known for throwing a touchdown pass to Golden Richards in Super Bowl XII.

Dallas fans had good reason to believe that they would never again see the likes of Tony Dorsett in Big D. The All-American from Pittsburgh, Dorsett darted into Dallas in 1977 and gave Tom Landry the running game he needed to lead the Cowboys to five NFC Championship games and two Super Bowls.

Dorsett racked up 12,739 yards in 11 seasons in Dallas, records that stood until Emmitt came along. And like Dorsett, Smith was acquired when Dallas moved up in the 1990 draft, trading Pittsburgh a choice first acquired from Minnesota in the famed Herschel Walker deal.

Walker and Dorsett played together briefly before Dorsett was traded to Denver to play for another former Dallas running back, Dan Reeves. Walker posted a 1,500-yard season in 1988, but it's largely forgotten in a rare era when the Cowboys weren't serious playoff contenders.

Enter Jimmy Johnson in 1989. Though his Dallas regime started with a 1–15 rock-bottom finish, Johnson began adding the necessary pieces for Dallas' next dynasty.

Troy Aikman was drafted that first season, and Emmitt came aboard the next. Michael Irvin was already in the fold, and when Johnson hired Norv Turner as offensive coordinator in 1991, all the pieces fell into place.

The "Triplets," the trio of Smith, Irvin, and Aikman, so named later under coach Barry Switzer's watch, dominated the NFL landscape through much of the nineties, leading Dallas to three titles in four seasons from 1992–1996. If

teams crowded the line of scrimmage to stop Emmitt, Aikman found Irvin in single coverage. If they doubled Irvin to limit Aikman's throws

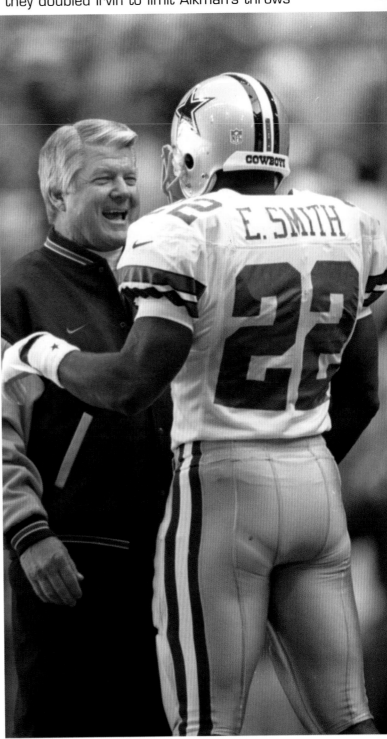

Smith repaid Johnson's faith in him by putting up Hall of Fame–type numbers during their years together.

downfield, a steady diet of Emmitt usually did the trick. And among all those great Dallas runners previously mentioned, Smith was the first Cowboy to lead the NFL in rushing.

Smith and Irvin roomed together toward the end of Smith's rookie season, and they became fast friends, though their personalities were very disparate. The quiet, unassuming Smith and the boastful, arrogant Irvin, both Florida natives, are forever linked with the Cowboys' successes in the nineties. Fans close their eyes and see them hugging in the end zone after another Dallas score, or in a more singular image, the two men embracing in the final minutes of the Cowboys' 38–28 loss in San Francisco in the 1994 NFC Championship game.

Emmitt later admitted he begged Irvin, "Don't leave me," that moment as the two wept while the season ended and Irvin headed into contract negotiations and possible free agency. Irvin was re-signed and a year later the Cowboys were back in the Super Bowl, beating Pittsburgh, a title that washed away a lot of bad memories for Dallas fans.

For the organization it was a title without Jimmy Johnson on the sideline, an important rite of passage for owner Jerry Jones. For fans it sealed an era that proved once again the Cowboys' place among the all-time great teams in league history. And the win over the Steelers was some consolation for two four-point losses in the Super Bowl to Pittsburgh in the seventies, when the Cowboys were arguably just those eight points away from being the team of that decade too.

And now, even as the brightness of the blue star on the helmet has waned in recent seasons on lackluster teams, Emmitt has given Cowboys fans reason to hold their heads high in his pursuit of Walter Payton's rushing record.

Barry Sanders was flashier. O. J. Simpson niftier. Jim Brown stronger. Eric Dickerson faster. But it's Emmitt who is now at the pinnacle after steadily chipping away all these years.

The consummate team guy, Smith also has three Super Bowl rings, another testament to his greatness. At an awards tribute this past summer, Smith broke down in tears thinking of his boyhood idol, Payton, and the chance to be considered alongside him as the greatest rusher ever in football. No one—not even demanding Dallas fans—have held Emmitt to a higher standard than Smith himself, who doggedly set his sights on this record when his NFL career began.

You're right there now, Emmitt. Thanks for the ride.

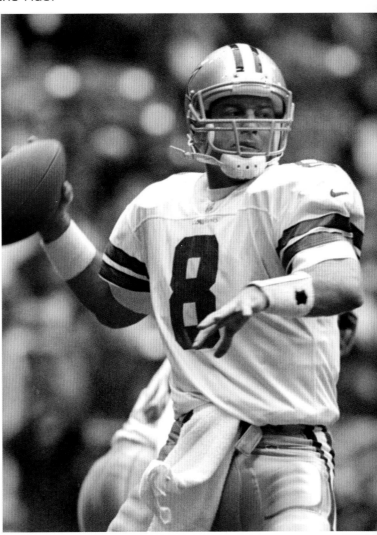

With Irvin (opposite page), Aikman (above), and Smith in place by the start of the decade, Dallas went on to become the undisputed team of the nineties.

The Rock

He held together one of sports' most fragile dynasties

Back in the nineties the Dallas Cowboys were at the height of their heyday—before their silver stars got tarnished, before mediocrity settled on America's Team like the scent of a dead skunk hanging over a hot August day.

On Monday afternoons in their locker room at Valley Ranch they basked in the aftermath of victory after victory. Once again the forces of evil had been turned back, and the Cowboys had triumphed with their smashmouth brand of football—their ability to jab Emmitt Smith at the opponent time and again, with only a few short passes for relief, forcing the defense to pack more and more men in the box until things opened up for Troy Aikman to find Michael Irvin.

THE ROCK

No other team in the NFL had a commitment to the running game like the Cowboys, and no one had a back like Emmitt Smith.

"I didn't need to see his resume," Jimmy Johnson explained of his trading up in the 1990 draft to get Smith, a three-time All-American out of the University of Florida. "I knew he was what Herschel Walker wasn't: a nifty runner. Emmitt also had a solid-as-a-rock personality and background. His parents are teachers. Emmitt is the kind of guy you can yell at on the practice field without worrying that you're going to crush him. He's too secure for that."

Over time, that rock-solid nature came to define Cowboy success. Eric Dickerson, a great running back with the Rams and the Colts, spoke in awe of Smith and Dallas. "That offense is designed to run it down your throat," he said. "Everything is based on the running game. You watch Emmitt; everything the Cowboys do is based on him.

"You don't see many teams that can run the football and just run it right down your throat and win the game when they have to."

It was the perfect balance to minimize the Buddy "Blowhard" Ryans of the world. On Sundays it was the defensive rush that made the Cowboys wary. But on Monday it was always the media crush that they had to face. Another week, another big game lay ahead, and there were questions to be answered. On one such Monday about two dozen reporters, armed with cameras, microphones, and notebooks, were waiting to catch the stars before a 2:00 P.M. team meeting.

Aikman suddenly appeared, eyed the gathering with his usual contempt, and, in a swift move, ducked the rush and slipped out of the room. It's instructive that Emmitt Smith took a different strategy—he waited until just a few minutes before the meeting to make his appearance, leaving the media a little frantic to get a quote.

The adulation for the Cowboys had always been a bit cloying. But the questions were much easier to answer in those good old days, before Irvin fell from grace and the organization stumbled under the weight of one public-relations disaster after another.

If only they all had been as rock solid as Emmitt.

I remember him that afternoon, grinning broadly, the diamond stud in his ear glistening in the TV lights. He offered up reassurances that his nagging hamstring was OK, which was very, very big news in Dallas at the time—bigger, say, than funding for supercollider projects or the latest polls from the governor's race.

This, after all, was football-crazy Texas in its greatest hour of gridiron glory. The Cowboys had just won two consecutive Super Bowls, and the only thing seemingly standing between them and a run of three or four of the suckers was good health. At the time, it all seemed to hinge on a hamstring. In retrospect, it now seems clear that it was far more fragile than that.

The team was driven by its trinity of offensive superstars—Smith, Aikman, and Irvin—who gave them a legitimate shot at becoming the first National Football League team to win three straight Super Bowls. The thought of this "three-peat" had fans in every corner of Cowboyland, which reaches far beyond the boundaries of the Lone Star state, twisting their intensity up another notch.

Yet as crazy as their fans were, no one wanted that third title—no one sensed the urgency more—than Emmitt himself. Time has proved that he was the heart of the team, the most dedicated, the one, above all of his fellow performers, who was willing to lay his heart on the line for each and every win.

The age of free agency had just dawned, meaning that players would come and go, all to the wherefores of the next big contract, surely threatening the Cowboys' opportunity to sustain a dynasty. Emmitt tried to make everyone around him aware of the circumstances.

"Since we're all together and this may be our last time, hell, let's make this the best run we've ever had," he said that day. "Let's do it the way it's supposed to be done. We have an opportunity for three Super Bowls, and I want to think this was the best team ever."

If only his teammates and coaches had heeded his sense of urgency; if only they hadn't welcomed the complacency. Further clouding the picture at the time was a controversial coaching change that had many observers thinking the Cowboys' glory train had been derailed. In a fit of barroom anger, owner Jerry Jones had fired immensely successful coach Johnson, despite the fact that they were old friends and teammates from the University of Arkansas—despite the fact that Johnson had just coached Dallas to two big trophies.

Stepping into the wake of this calamity were new head coach Barry Switzer and new offensive coordinator Ernie Zampese, both of whom grinned

THE ROCK

and guffawed at the pressure. Could the newly rebuilt defense stand up to the challenges week after week? Could the offense stay healthy? Could Switzer provide the discipline that a team soaked in adulation would need?

The circumstances themselves were enough to drive a wedge between the churlish Aikman and his back-slapping new head coach, whose last coaching experience had been watching the disintegration of the University of Oklahoma program he had guided to national prominence. If Switzer seemed a little confused at early key moments on the Cowboys' sideline, Aikman and Smith had been there before—so rather than wait for a coaching decision, they simply took charge.

If Switzer chaffed at these or other small indignities wrought by doing the bidding of Jones, the coach was a master at not showing it. Amazingly, he seemed unconcerned that he would surely be the fall guy if the team chemistry fell apart. Aikman predicted, "There will come a time when Barry will have to take a stand."

Yes, the quarterback was, for the record, setting the responsibility squarely on the coach's shoulders. Not that Aikman didn't do everything possible, including playing through a series of career-threatening head injuries that would leave him struggling with bouts of memory lapses for seasons to come.

Free agency had brought the loss of John Gesek and Kevin Gogan from the offensive line; coordinator Norv Turner had departed for a head coaching job in Washington; and tackle Erik Williams had suffered season-ending injuries in an auto accident. Who knows how far Emmitt could have taken them if only that line had stayed healthy through the key moments?

In any event, Aikman found himself yelling at a rookie lineman here or there that season for missed assignments that resulted in the run getting stuffed or the quarterback getting leveled by the pass rush. For the immensely popular Irvin the main adversity wasn't injury or even the zone and double-coverage defenses that were determined to take away the Cowboys' long-ball threat. Mainly, his struggle each evening came down to which delicious elements of the Dallas nightlife he wanted to sample. After all, the choices were bodacious.

That didn't mean that Irvin didn't have his on-field problems in those days. The 1994 season was a month old before the big-playing, big-talking receiver had caught his first touchdown pass, mainly because of the defenses gearing their efforts to shutting him down. The circumstances had tested the 6'2", 208-pound Irvin, who in college nicknamed himself "Playmaker." There were early

season scenes from the Dallas sideline with him storming about and swearing that he was being overlooked in the offense.

"I don't tolerate that," Aikman reacted angrily. "Mike should be wise enough to know we'll get him the ball."

Outside of these histrionics, the Cowboys seemed their smiling, assured selves in 1994, the darlings of Dallas. Behind the scenes the forces that would take them down were gathering momentum. On the surface only one question seemed to matter: could the team's offensive superstars withstand the battering that opposing defenses subjected them to week after week?

"That's something I can't worry about," Smith said, "because if I do, I end up shortchanging myself."

That comment, in itself, sums up the toughness, the mindset, behind his unprecedented durability. For membership into the elite club of competitors that includes men like Jerry Rice or Michael Jordan or John Stockton or Karl Malone, a star has to shrug off the injuries that would sideline men with weaker wills. Emmitt's determination gives him residence in that elite group.

Aikman's problems centered on a series of six concussions dating back through several seasons and their long-term effects. Get enough concussions and you risk permanent brain damage, doctors had repeatedly warned pro football players. That fall Cardinals linebacker Wilber Marshall sent Aikman to the sideline with a hammering blow to the chin that caused yet another concussion.

Like Smith, the concussion-prone Aikman put his career in jeopardy during his quest for three Super Bowl titles.

THE ROCK

"I find myself forgetting things," he later revealed. "I don't know if it's like anyone else forgetting things, or if it's the result of being hit in the head too much. I forget having entire conversations with people."

Despite the risks, Aikman had missed only one game, then rushed back to his starting role the next week, much as Smith had made a point of battering through a playoff win the previous December against the Giants despite a separated shoulder that would require off-season surgery. That, as much as anything, separated the Cowboys from the competition. In addition to their bountiful talent and competitiveness, the Dallas offensive stars had always shown a ready willingness to risk their long-term health to keep winning.

Before injuries and off-field distractions derailed the careers of Aikman (.8) and Irvin (.88), respectively, the pair teamed with Smith (.22) to become one of football's most prolific offensive machines of all time.

The immense risks seemed to steep Aikman's resentment of the underprepared Switzer. The situation intensified with their failure to win their third consecutive championship that winter, their hopes of a dynasty derailed by injuries and a lack of depth. They were simply too beat up to outlast the competition in the playoffs.

In the wake of that disappointment came the biggest test of Emmitt's competitiveness. After all, he already had two Super Bowl rings. Would he grow complacent? Or would he roar back, bringing the Cowboys with him?

Smith's 1995 season was the giant reason the Cowboys claimed another Super Bowl title. He rushed for 1,773 yards (a 4.7 average) and a league-record 25 TDs. In the NFC Championship game against Green Bay, he rolled up 150 yards rushing and three TDs, two of them in the fourth quarter with Smith leading a Cowboy surge to erase a 27–24 Packer lead and produce a 38–27 Dallas victory.

He scored two more touchdowns in Super Bowl XXX as the Cowboys outlasted the Steelers, 27–17.

For that brief instant, Jones and Switzer were vindicated. God had blessed Aikman, Smith, Irvin, and Associates with three titles in four seasons, and the future seemed Texas-sized and packed with limousines, longnecks, and gorgeous blondes.

But it all disintegrated just a few weeks later when Dallas police busted into a Marriott Residence Inn room and caught Irvin in a drugs and sex scandal that would blast the good times away like a twister rolling in off the nearby plain. Eventually, the whole thing would be laid at Switzer's feet, driven by Aikman's haunting prediction that, someday, the coach would indeed have to take a stand. Switzer would have gladly done so, if he had only known which one to take.

For Emmitt and his teammates the 1996 campaign was one of frustration. His average rushing yardage per game dipped below 4.0, and the season ended with observers questioning

Switzer's short but eventful tenure in Dallas included the team's third Super Bowl title in four years.

whether his best days were behind him—this despite the fact that he gained better than 1,200 yards that year and scored 12 touchdowns. Part of the problem was a pitiful Dallas passing game that meant every time Smith ran the ball he was greeted by an eight-man defensive front.

Some would say their troubles were to be expected considering they spent the year embroiled in one controversy after another. "We lost Michael Irvin for five games, Kelvin Martin and Kevin Williams were hobbled by injuries, Jay Novacek was gone, Eric Bjornson was limping on two sprained ankles, and Deion [Sanders] never got into the flow," Aikman said. "Our offense was an embarrassment and I was horrible."

Aikman pointed out that a dozen other NFL teams would kill for a 10–6 finish. In Dallas, though, the expectations were dramatically steeper.

The image of the Cowboys in the final hours of the 1996 season wasn't pretty. Contained by the Carolina Panthers' intimidating defense in the

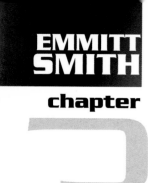

THE ROCK

NFC semifinals, the Dallas offense was short on receivers and answers. Throughout it all, their one consistent weapon remained Emmitt Smith.

"We couldn't throw the ball last year when teams stopped our running game," Aikman admitted as the team headed into the 1997 campaign. "Unlike last year, I think we'll be able to throw the ball without any problems. Emmitt is healthy again and if teams decide to load up against him this time, they'll have to pay the price."

The Emmitt machine got an overhaul that off-season—surgery to correct problems with bone spurs and chips. He, too, seemed eager heading into the 1997 season, if not to claim redemption, at least to bash those who suggested he needed it.

No sooner had the Cowboys issued new vows to clean up their act for 1997—and hired former great Calvin Hill (father of the NBA's Grant Hill) as a consultant to help them do it—than Switzer was caught toting an unlicensed gun into an airport. Considering the team's public-relations nightmares, Jones was tempted to fire him but settled instead for a league-record $75,000 fine.

That was followed by a charge by Nate Newton's former girlfriend that he had sexually assaulted her (a grand jury later declined to indict him on the charge). If nothing else, the incidents emphasized to Jones and his minions that they must find a way to scrub the tarnish off the team's silver stars. The fastest way to accomplish that would be a return to championship contention in 1997. Anything less meant that the proceedings would play out in the Texas media like a smarmy B-grade western. Heaven knows the city had seen enough of prime-time soap operas.

One of the keys to turning the thing around included finding some way around the team's severe decline in manpower. Since the end of the 1996 campaign the Cowboys had seen seven unrestricted free agents leave for other teams. In addition, back injuries caused tight end Novacek and defensive end Charles Haley, both former Pro Bowlers, to retire.

The free-agent losses included both kickers (punter John Jett to Detroit and place-kicker Chris Boniol to Philadelphia). Even worse, Darrin Smith, the team's most effective linebacker, headed to Philadelphia, and two other starters, wide receiver Kevin Williams and safety George Teague, also went to other teams. In the five years since the NFL had been forced to allow free agency, the Cowboys had lost 33 players, including 14 starters and three Pro Bowlers.

Even as the situation deteriorated around him, Smith would remain the rock—the one constant for Cowboy fans. "God put

Emmitt Smith here to run with the football," Irvin once explained.

He had more than lived up to that billing since the Cowboys made him the 17th overall player taken in the 1990 draft. He had claimed four rushing titles, a passel of Pro Bowl appearances, and awards as both the league's regular-season and Super Bowl Most Valuable Player.

Many considered him the Cowboys' most essential ingredient. "It's been proven," offered Green Bay defensive end Reggie White. "They've won without Troy. They never win without Emmitt."

Former 49ers coach Bill Walsh once said admirably that the 5'9", 209-pound Smith "is incomparable to any in the game today. He has a combination of speed, quickness, elusiveness, power, and competitiveness that is unmatched."

It was during that glory run in the mid-nineties that Smith first admitted that his accomplishments and the accolades had led him to think about catching Walter Payton as the NFL's all-time leading rusher. Heading into the 1997 season Smith had 10,160 career yards, ahead of Payton's totals at the same point in his career.

But catching Payton would be far from easy, Smith had acknowledged in 1994. "If anybody has a chance, it's me. When I won the first rushing title, people wondered if I was for real and if I could do it again. Then I won the second and they thought maybe I was for real. Then the third one made me legitimate. But now people want to know this: how long can Emmitt Smith be on top? I think I can be there a long time."

Time would reveal that Smith coveted the high expectations in Dallas—in fact, they were part of what drove him to compete.

He spent the remainder of his career seeking to chase away the demons and return his Cowboys to the good old days, when Sunday afternoons were for winning and reporters' questions would hang in the air, fat and oh-so-easy to answer, when the whole wide world seemed sweet as barbecue.

It didn't work out that way, of course. On many game days, it seemed that Smith was left to shoulder the burden alone, which he did with a dignity that brings to mind the great Payton. That's why NFL fans will always think of them together, way out there ahead of the pack, straining to gain just a little more ground.

Just what you'd expect of a rock.

The Long Shot

Against all odds, Smith rates at the top of the all-time list

It grew out of gross behavior, this matter of being a running back. You see, football evolved from English soccer way back in the 19th century, and back then the Brits were infinitely annoyed with Americans because they kept picking up the damn ball and running with it, which was a no-no.

"Don't you Yanks have the common decency to obey the rules?" the Brits used to say.

"Yes," the Americans would reply, "we understand the rules. But running with the ball is so natural. Why don't you just pick that sucker up and head for the goal?"

THE LONG SHOT

4

We've come a long way since those first glimmering days of American football. Now we have high-tech offenses and strong-armed quarterbacks to fling the ball 60 yards upfield. But the essence of the sport remains the running game—the ability of a very special back to take the pigskin and (choose your verb) dive, rush, smash, sprint, cut, glide, shift, or shag his way upfield for a gain. That has been—and always will be—the safest, simplest way to advance the ball.

One of the game's earliest runners, Jim Thorpe still ranks among the best of all time.

Faced with that basic assignment, it didn't take the game's early coaches long to discover the prototype for a great runner. Strong, swift, shifty, durable, someone able to run over or around the opposition.

It was Jim Thorpe's good fortune to possess all of those characteristics and come along just as early rule changes, including the forward pass, had opened up the game from its early "three yards and a cloud of dust." Because of that, we think of him as the first great running back.

A two-time All American at Carlisle Indian School in Pennsylvania, Thorpe went on to a long, distinguished pro career. He had the speed and shiftiness to get around tacklers, but he also had the size and strength to run over them, which is what he preferred to do because of his great competitive nature. He so loved to smash a tackler, in fact, that toward the end of his career, as his prowess waned, he was accused of fashioning a pair of hard leather shoulder pads and lacing them with metal rivets, just so he could still deliver that special pop to defenders.

The next great link in the evolutionary chain of the ball carrier, Red Grange, the "Galloping Ghost," emerged at the University of Illinois in the twenties. While the pro game was struggling to gather a fan following, Big Ten college football was regularly pulling in 80,000 spectators in that first great Golden Age of sport, and Grange, also known as the "Wheaton Iceman," was the primary attraction.

It was also the age of the great sportswriters, and Grantland Rice composed prose poems for newspaper leads lionizing Grange's graceful, deceptive style: "There are two shapes now moving/Two ghosts that drift and glide/And which of them to tackle/Each rival must decide/They shift with spectral swiftness/Across the swarded range/And one of them's a shadow/And one of them is Grange."

This elusive style, in fact, stirred up such a media frenzy that the Chicago Bears signed Grange as soon as he completed his last game at Illinois in the late fall of 1925, just in time for him to join the team at Thanksgiving. The press claimed the move was a crass show of professionalism, but Grange brought his fan following to the struggling NFL.

Many franchises were fighting for survival until the Bears launched a season-ending Grange exhibition tour that filled every stadium it visited. The exhibition was so successful that the Bears launched a second tour in Miami on Christmas day that saw Grange play 19 games in 17 cities in just 66 days.

The pace left him exhausted and injured (his career would be shortened by injuries), but there was no question that Grange was the running back who popularized pro football and headed it toward financial prosperity. Because of his exploding popularity, Grange was invited to the White House to visit President Calvin Coolidge. "This is Red Grange, who plays with the Bears," said a senator who introduced the Galloping Ghost to the president. "Coolidge shook my hand," Grange later recalled, "and said, 'Nice to meet you, young man. I've always liked animal acts.' "

Coolidge, of course, was revealing that he knew absolutely nothing about pro football (not very many people did back in the twenties). Yet, in a sense, he had managed to sum up the very essence of the sport. "This is a game for madmen," Vince Lombardi, the great Green Bay Packers coach, once observed. Especially the running backs.

Since its earliest beginnings, the NFL has been populated by strange, hard-drinking, hard-driving men who possess unhealthy levels of testosterone. Men who smile toothlessly at the idea of smashmouth football. Men like rebel running back Joe Don Looney, who used to make a show of eating light bulbs and jumping out of third-floor windows. A wacko power back, he played for a variety of teams, most of which

THE LONG SHOT

refused to keep him for more than a few weeks because he was so insane. For example, he used to like to sleep in cemeteries, "because it's so peaceful there."

Hall of Famer John Riggins was another major maniac. He held out from the Jets in 1973. When he finally signed a contract, he showed up shirtless with leather pants and a Mohawk haircut. "Damndest sight you ever saw," said Jets coach Weeb Ewbank. "He had that Mohawk haircut and he was stripped to the waist and he was wearing leather pants and a derby hat with a feather in it. It must have been what the sale of Manhattan Island looked like."

It should be pointed out that players didn't have to be crazy to play the position of running back, but it sure seemed to help.

Another early prototype, the big, swift back, also wore a Bears uniform and was more than a bit loony. Bronko Nagurski, a 6'2", 225-pounder, was a dominant ball carrier during the early thirties. There are many legends about his size, strength, and toughness, but perhaps the most indicative was the story that he once collided with a policeman's horse standing on the sidelines and knocked the poor beast out cold. When you consider that Bronk was wearing only a leather helmet, that's quite a bash.

Gale Sayers

"I remember one game," Bears coach George Halas once recalled, "his head was down, charging like a bull. Nagurski blasted through two tacklers at the goal line as if they were a pair of old-time saloon doors, through the end zone, and full speed into the brick retaining wall behind it. The sickening thud reverberated throughout the stadium."

Staggering, Nagurski came over to the bench and told Halas, "That last guy really gave me a good lick."

Another time Nagurski was horsing around with some friends on the second floor of a hotel room when he crashed through a window and fell into the busy street below. "What happened?" asked a police officer who rushed up to check on the commotion.

"I don't know," Nagurski replied as he got groggily to his feet. "I just got here myself."

The emergence of the NFL after World War II brought a new age of running backs, the kind who could thrill crowds with their ability to "break one." There was a special magic about a ball carrier's slashing through the line of scrimmage and into the open field that could force a collective gasp from spectators. It's the same kind of thrill that follows the special crack of the bat at the launching of a home run or the grunt of the rim on a monster slam dunk.

Yet, in another sense, those other sports involve lesser feats because the ball carrier faces a much more severe physical challenge in a climate that is far more threatening. Each line buck, each cut against the grain, offers the potential for major injury. The constant battering reduces the average running back's career to only four seasons.

That makes the special talents and durability of the game's greatest ball carriers all the more remarkable. Some had fancy gliding styles. Others used bull power. Some were slashers. Whether it was Jim Brown's special mix of power and speed, Gale Sayers' fluid elusiveness, or Walter Payton's strength and agility, great running backs have come to be evaluated on an array of factors, including the success of their teams, their statistics, their durability, their performances in big games, and their contributions to the fabric of the sport.

Emmitt Smith's place in the pantheon of great running backs has always generated more than a bit of discussion. If you were to believe many of the recruiting specialists who evaluated his talent coming out of high school in Pensacola, Florida, he lacked the merit for consideration. "Emmitt isn't a franchise player," wrote one talent scout. "He's a lugger, not a runner. Sportswriters blew him all out of proportion."

Smith simply used his play to answer such talk. His first start as a freshman at the University of Florida brought a new Gator single-game rushing record: 224 yards on 39 carries. He's been consistently reliable ever since, always helping his team to move the chains, not with flashy open-field running or monster touchdown runs, but with the ability to relentlessly attack and probe a defense.

In person he seems compact, even too small to be a superstar. But there's the vision, the balance, the surprising strength in breaking tackles—characteristics that have made him the most consistently effective weapon in NFL history.

Jim Brown

For 11 straight NFL seasons, from 1991 to 2001, he gained better than 1,000 yards rushing, a record that eclipsed the best efforts of both Payton and Barry Sanders, who maintained that pace for 10 seasons.

There are critics who overlook this prodigious productivity to complain that Emmitt has lacked elusiveness and style. Former teammate Nate Newton once took exception to that line of thought. "When Emmitt needs to make you miss, he can make anybody miss," Newton said. "And when he needs to run over you, he can do that, too."

THE LONG SHOT

chapter 4

Regardless, Smith has always insisted that such analysis or stats or even records "don't tell you what kind of football player you are. My talent came from God. What I add is my desire. I have great desire."

That desire has made him pro football's all-time rushing leader. It has also made him one of the three greatest backs in the history of the game. What follows is a ranking of the NFL's greatest backs that leaves the game's dominant backs tied for top honors.

Walter Payton

1. (three-way tie)

Jim Brown: Probably the toughest competitor in the history of the game. An All-American in both football and lacrosse at Syracuse University, the 6'2", 238-pound Brown was the NFL's Rookie of the Year in 1957. An eight time All-Pro, he led the league in rushing every year except one during his nine-year career and was voted Player of the Year in 1958, 1963, and 1965.

He retired in 1966 at the age of 30, but by then he had already amassed 12,312 yards rushing on 2,359 carries. He scored 106 rushing touchdowns and another 20 receiving.

Emmitt Smith: The centerpiece in a Dallas Cowboys offense that won three Super Bowls, the 5'9", 209-pound Smith rushed for 8,956 yards in his first six seasons and scored 100 touchdowns (96 rushing, 4 on passes). From there he would plug on, disproving naysayers who said he lacked the discipline to break Payton's all-time record. Heading into the 2002 season, Emmitt ranked as the all-time rushing touchdown leader with 148, 25 ahead of Marcus Allen in second place.

Walter Payton: Before Smith, Payton set the standard in all-time rushing yardage with 16,726 yards. The 5'10", 203-pound Payton came out of Jackson State in 1975 to join the Bears. Over his 13-year career he rushed for more than 1,000 yards in 10 seasons and rushed for 110 touchdowns. A fine blocker and receiver, the superbly conditioned Payton was the league's Player of the Year in 1985. His nickname, "Sweetness," belied just how tough he was.

2. Barry Sanders: This guy was Fred Astaire in cleats. He won the Heisman as a junior at Oklahoma State in 1988, then hopped to the Detroit Lions, where in his first seven seasons he rushed for 10,172 yards and 72 touchdowns while averaging a super 4.9 yards per carry.

Emmitt Smith

Sanders could have made a serious challenge for the all-time record but retired abruptly after the 1998 season following a snit with Lions coach Bobby Ross. He quit after rolling to 15,269 yards over 10 seasons.

Barry Sanders

THE LONG SHOT

3. Tony Dorsett: In many regards he was the Lamborghini of running backs, with a sleek style, great vision, and speed aplenty. A two-time All-American at the University of Pittsburgh, Dorsett claimed the 1976 Heisman, then followed it up with 1977 NFL Rookie of the Year honors as a Dallas Cowboy. "Touchdown Tony" rang up more than 1,000 yards on the ground in each of his first six pro seasons and concluded his playing days with the Denver Broncos in 1988 with a career total of 12,379 yards.

4. Eric Dickerson: At 6'3", 230 pounds, this guy had rare size and speed. He came out of Southern Methodist to earn Rookie of the Year honors with the Los Angeles Rams in 1982 and was named NFC Player of the Year the next season with a league-

Eric Dickerson

eading 1,808 yards rushing. He rushed for more than 1,000 yards in seven consecutive seasons, a record. In 1984 he set the league's single-season rushing record with 2,105 yards. He again led the league in rushing as a Ram in 1986, then moved on to the Indianapolis Colts and again led the league in 1988. For all of his grand totals, however, his career was marked by clashes with coaches and management. A five-time All Pro, he retired in 1993 with better than 13,000 career yards.

5. O. J. Simpson: Forget the white Bronco for a moment if you can and look at just his football career. The 6'1", 212-pound Simpson won the Heisman Trophy at Southern Cal in 1969, then moved on to the Buffalo Bills, where he was a part-time player until moving into the starting lineup in 1972 and becoming a star. In 1973 he became the first back to rush for more than 2,000 yards in a season. He finished his career with the 49ers in 1978 and 1979 and amassed career totals of 11,236 yards and 76 touchdowns.

6. Franco Harris: Nothing fancy here, just power. The 6'2", 225-pound Harris was a blocking fullback at Penn State who found stardom in the NFL. He was a key factor for four Pittsburgh Steeler Super Bowl championship teams and was MVP of Super Bowl IX, when he gained 158 yards on 34 carries. He gained 12,120 yards and scored 91 rushing TDs in 13 years as a pro.

7. Thurman Thomas: This 5'10", 198-pounder out of Oklahoma State gained 9,729 yards over his first eight NFL seasons. His play was a key factor in the Buffalo Bills reaching four Super Bowls, but critics charge it was also a factor in the Bills losing all four championship games.

Terrell Davis

8. John Riggins: The 6'2", 230-pound Riggo came out of the University of Kansas to the New York Jets in 1971 and jumped to the Washington Redskins in 1976 as a free agent. The big hoss in the Redskins' single-back offense, Riggins was named Most Valuable Player of Super Bowl XVII after he rushed for 166 yards in 38 attempts to lead Washington over Miami. He was named the league's Player of the Year in 1983 after rushing for 1,347 yards and a record 24 touchdowns. Over his 14-year career he rushed for 11,352 yards and 104 touchdowns.

9. Terrell Davis: The Most Valuable Player of Super Bowl XXXIII, Davis became only the third back in NFL history to rush for more than 2,000 yards in a season in 1998 when he tallied 2,008 for Denver. A knee injury forced an early end to his career.

THE LONG SHOT

10. Earl Campbell: This 5'11", 230-pounder could hammer defenses inside with his power, then turn on his speed to break into the open for long gains. He won the Heisman at the University of Texas in 1977, then moved to the Houston Oilers and led the NFL in rushing for four straight seasons, from 1977 to 1981, until injuries began to limit his playing time. He retired in 1985, having gained 9,407 yards over his career and scored 74 touchdowns.

Marshall Faulk

11. Gale Sayers: A brilliant open-field runner out of the University of Kansas, Sayers went to the Chicago Bears and earned Rookie of the Year honors in 1965. He led the league in rushing in 1966 and 1969. Knee injuries forced his early retirement in 1971, but not before he had rung up 9,435 career yards and 56 touchdowns.

12. Marcus Allen: Although he suffered through several seasons of misuse as a Los Angeles Raider, the 6'2", 210-pound Allen gained 10,908 yards rushing and scored 103 touchdowns in a 14-year pro career. At Southern Cal he set an NCAA single-season rushing record with 2,432 yards.

13. Ottis Anderson: He set a rookie rushing record with the St. Louis Cardinals in 1979 (1,605 yards), then followed that with four 1,000-yard seasons over the next five years. He was traded to New York in 1986 and gained 1,023 yards in 1989. He was named the MVP of Super Bowl XXV with 102 yards rushing in the Giants' 20–19 win over Buffalo.

14. Marshall Faulk: Considered one of the best backs in the modern game, Faulk has rushed for better than 1,000 yards for eight straight seasons for Indiana and then the St. Louis Rams, the team he led to victory in Super Bowl XXXIV.

15. Jerome Bettis: A big back for the Rams and then the Steelers, Bettis has also racked up eight seasons of rushing for more than 1,000 yards as "The Bus."

16. Roger Craig: He was a power player for three San Francisco 49er Super Bowl championship teams. Craig is the first back in history to gain more than 1,000 yards each

Earl Campbell

rushing and receiving in one season (1985) and owns the single-season record for receptions by a running back with 92.

17. Herschel Walker: If you count his yardage in the United States Football League, Walker has gained more rushing real estate than any human being. As it is, his 8,122 yards rushing and 60 touchdowns in 10 NFL seasons ain't bad. Plus he has another 4,621 yards and 19 more touchdowns receiving.

chapter

4

THE LONG SHOT

18. Jim Taylor: At 215 pounds, this LSU product didn't have the size to play pro fullback, but he was a fixture on Vince Lombardi's Green Bay Packer teams. For three straight seasons, 1960–62, he gained more than 1,000 yards and led the league in rushing in 1962. For his career he gained 8,597 yards and scored 96 touchdowns.

19. Larry Csonka: He built a reputation as a hard runner and dependable blocker while leading the Miami Dolphins to their glory seasons in the early seventies. He was named the MVP of Super Bowl VIII after gaining 145 yards on 33 carries to power Miami past Minnesota for the championship. A 6'3", 235-pounder, he rushed for 8,081 yards in 11 NFL seasons.

20. Steve Van Buren: This five-time All Pro graduated from LSU in 1943 and went on to power the Philadelphia Eagles to two NFL titles. He led the league in rushing in 1945, 1947, 1948, and 1949 and gained 195 yards rushing in the Eagles' 1949 championship win over the Rams.

21. Leroy Kelly: He led the league in rushing in 1967 and 1968 and was also 1968 league MVP with 1,269 yards rushing and 16 touchdowns.

22. Joe Perry: Led the league in rushing 1953–1954 with the San Francisco 49ers. Amassed 8,378 yards in 14 seasons. If you consider his All America Football Conference years with San Francisco, Perry actually totaled 9,723 yards in 16 seasons.

23. Gerald Riggs: Over a 10-year pro career he gained 8,188 yards. In 1985 he led the NFC in rushing with 1,719 yards.

24. Bronko Nagurski, Red Grange, and Jim Thorpe: These three old timers who tied for 24th on our list are cited for their many combined contributions to the game.

25. Edgerrin James, Ricky Watters, and Curtis Martin: Similarly, these three modern backs round out the list at No. 25 for amassing substantial yardage with the potential to move up on the all-time standings.